3xE Discipleship–Discipler Version:

Exaltation, Edification, Evangelism

Books by Paul J. Bucknell

Overcoming Anxiety: Finding Peace, Discovering God

Life in the Spirit! Experiencing the Fullness of Christ

Reaching Beyond Mediocrity: Being an Overcomer

The Life Core: Discovering the Heart of Great Training

The Godly Man: When God Touches a Man's Life

Redemption Through the Scriptures

Godly Beginnings for the Family

Principles and Practices of Biblical Parenting

Building a Great Marriage

Christian Premarital Counseling Manual for Counselors

Relational Discipleship: Cross Training

Running the Race: Overcoming Sexual Lusts

The Bible Teaching Commentary on Genesis

The Bible Teaching Commentary on Romans

3xE Discipleship Booklets

Life Transformation: A Monthly Devotional on Romans 12:9-21

Book of Romans: Bible Studies

Book of Ephesians: Bible Studies

Abiding in Christ: Walking with Jesus

Inductive Bible Studies in Titus

1 Peter Bible Study Questions: Living in a Fallen World

Take Your Next Step into Ministry

The Lord Your Healer: Discover Him and Find His Healing

Training Leaders for Ministry

Satan's Four Stations: The Destroyer is Destroyed

Study Questions for Jonah: Understanding the Heart of God

Our Digital Libraries include these books as well as slides, handouts, audio/videos, and much more at: www.foundationsforfreedom.net

3xE Discipleship–
Discipler Version:

Exaltation, Edification, Evangelism

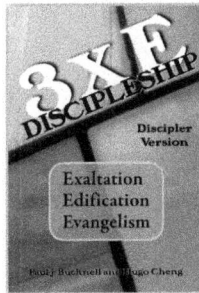

Paul J. Bucknell

Hugo Cheng

3xE Discipleship–Discipler Version: Exaltation, Edification, Evangelism
Copyright ©2016 Paul J. Bucknell and Hugo Cheng

Printed paperback:
ISBN-10: 1-61993-075-7
ISBN-13: 978-1-61993-075-9

Also Digital e-book
ISBN-10: 1-61993-076-5
ISBN-13: 978-1-61993-076-6

3xE Discipleship–Disciple Version
ISBN-13: 978-1-61993-077-3 (Paperback)
ISBN-13: 978-1-61993-078-0 (Digital)

www.foundationsforfreedom.net
Pittsburgh, PA 15212 USA

The NASB version is used unless otherwise stated.
New American Standard Bible ©1960, 1995 used by permission,
Lockman Foundation www.lockman.org.

Dedication

God is so gracious to not only save us from our sins and bring us to Himself, but to incorporate us in His amazing work of nuturing new believers. Our hearts are touched that such an astonishing work is placed into our hands. Praise be to God!

Table of Contents

Preface

Discipleship is a crucial part of the care and development of Christians, new and old. As a pastor I realized that we needed to implement a discipleship movement in our church. Back in the 1990s, I found that only student ministries published their discipleship materials and that they were lacking in three key areas:

(1) The college discipleship manuals didn't connect students to the local church. In the church I was pastoring there were many students, and I found that the strongest ones were those who connected to the church. When I realized that the college discipleship materials did not teach about the importance of the local church, I became concerned because those materials were disorienting young believers and disregarding a basic discipleship principle.

(2) Discipleship materials are often self-focused. Believers are typically trained to focus on their own spiritual lives rather than to gain a Christ-perspective, which is the only thing that allows a deep and powerful focus on others to develop.

(3) These resources were not flexible. As a teacher, I believe each discipler needs to teach according to their style and yet stay focused on discussing key issues.

3xE is a one-on-one 7-week discipleship course designed for new believers or those starting anew in their Christian faith. The 3xE shows the importance of the local church as well as provides a consistent emphasis to shift the focus from what the disciple profits to what he or she can give as Christ's disciple. Having two versions, a Discipler and Disciplee, give us much more flexibility, enabling the teacher to have notes, teaching points, and key verses but also the freedom to substitute Bible versions, teaching points, etc., so that the Discipler can focus on the needs of the disciple.

My vision is that Christians would take seriously the call to train up disciples, just as our Lord commanded the church in Matthew 28:18-20. We hope this booklet will provide a solid, biblical, and practical path to enable you, and those around you, to make disciples.

Paul J. Bucknell

Pittsburgh, PA USA.

An Introduction

Discipleship is one Christian helping another Christian grow in knowing, following, and serving Jesus Christ. Every Christian should be able to disciple others. Whether you think you can or not, you are called to be a discipler.

The main value of discipleship training rests on the growth of the relationship between the discipler and disciple rather than on the content of this booklet. Because of this, we move toward the goal of passing on a God-centered vision and passion.

The 3xE discipleship plan helps you focus on others: God, other Christians, and non-Christians. At its core, 3xE is all about love. We want to pass on the motivating and empowering love of God to each of Christ's disciples.

Christ's love calls us all from complacency into active spheres of worship, brotherhood, and community. This is the backbone of our discipleship training:

> • **We exalt God** for His Name's sake rather than for ourselves. When we seek what we like rather than what God desires, our worship of the holy God denigrates into the worship of self. We must carefully search both the scriptures and our hearts to make sure that all that that we do is done in a fashion that pleases Him.

> • **We edify others** in our obedience and love for God. Sure, we like being fed and taught, but a higher purpose calls us to bless our brothers and sisters in Christ. Further, we should be genuinely excited to see God use our spiritual gifts to benefit others.

> • **We evangelize others** in obedient and loving service to God. We dare not allow ourselves to interfere in this process by protecting our fears, feelings, and pride. Reaching the lost is the responsibility of each disciple's life and purpose.

3xE, therefore, serves as a strategic resource allowing a church or individual to make and empower their disciples to make more disciples!

Usage of 3xE Resources

1. One-on-one is the ideal "class size"; that is, one mentor and one disciple. The two should be of the same sex. Three is sometimes okay. Remember that you are building friendships too.

2. Before starting, ask the student to commit to seven sessions for about 1 1/2 to 2 hours each. Home assignments will usually require 30 minutes to complete. Please start with the Discipleship Covenant, which is included in both the student and teacher's edition.

3. Before starting, mention that your goal is to make him or her a disciple-maker. Share your plan of having he or she, after these sessions, to join you when discipling another person so that he or she can more comfortably learn how to disciple others.

4. Each class should start and end with prayer. Try to build some mutual accountability into your sharing and thus further build each other up in the Lord.

5. Teachers should review what needs to be taught before class. They should be fresh and eager to study God's Word. Remember that the most important lesson to be passed on is your vivacious love for God, fellow Christians, and non-Christians.

6. There are two editions of 3xE.

There is plenty of space in the Disciple version, and verses from the Bible are intentionally absent. This is to allow the discipler to use verses and versions he or she thinks are most appropriate, and to provoke the disciple to engage their minds as they record important information. Remind them to take notes! This way they can refer to this booklet later, to help them when they disciple others.

The teacher's edition is packed full of notes and Bible verses. In fact, the best teacher's edition is your old student one (if you have it) with all your personal notes, but the discipler's edition can help fill in where you may lack confidence or knowledge, and it will certainly help when you are preparing for a session with a student disciple. Most of these teacher notes are in a smaller italic font.

7. 3xE is designed with the local church in mind, making its approach a stark contrast to most other discipleship materials. A Christian's success will largely have to do with how well they have integrated into the local church. The Lord's goal for them is to make disciples. The mentor might need to help the student to find and settle in a good church.

8. The material is free to use and adapt in God-honoring ways. Please send a copy with suggestions for any improvements! Give each graduate a teacher's edition upon completion of the course. May God bless your efforts! (info@foundationsforfreedom.net)

9. Both Discipler and Disciplee should already be genuinely saved. The mentor models Christ's heart and mind, providing a easy path for the disciplee to follow after Christ. Each day is an adventure with the Lord.

Have a great adventure growing in Christ together!

Prayer Journal

The discipler is to have the disciple start a prayer journal. The disciple is to record their prayer requests and keep track of them, writing the date when they are answered. Though we provide a sheet for this in the booklet, it probably is better that the disciple has a separate notebook for this.

Date asked	Prayer Request	Date Answered

Daily Prayer

This is a simple and popular way to remind them of the basic components of prayer. Do stress the relationship side of prayer with God. Prayer is bi-directional, as it is in a simple two-way conversation. Have them pray out loud even if they start with simple sentences.

A.C.T.S.

- Adoration (Psalm 139, 145)

- Confession (Psalm 139:23-24; 1 John 1:9)

- Thanksgiving (Psalm 100)

- Supplication (request for specific needs)

  – Pray for protection from Satan

  – Pray for victory over sins

  – Pray to be a channel of blessing

Discipleship Pledge

We encourage faithfulness by this simple pledge to meet together seven times. It helps them understand and develop faithfulness, seeing what they can reap from such times together. Remember, if they are going to disciple others, they will need to be convinced of the value of these meeting times.

Discipleship Pledge

I, _____ covenant with

_____ before God to begin

and finish this discipleship process.

I agree to:

- Attend all seven sessions of training.
- Complete all my assignments on time.
- Pray for my partner and the training sessions weekly.
- Apply what I learned daily.
- Respect my discipler and be open and honest with him/her.
- Pass on the vision and passion by discipling at least one other person with this material.

Signed: _____

Date: _____

Session #1 Introduction to 3xE

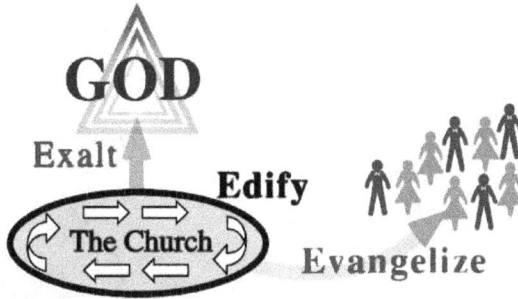

❖ Welcome to the family

Discipleship is more than the passing on of knowledge; it is the experience, attitude, and activity of passing it on. It's a lifestyle.

> Get somewhat acquainted with each person in the discipleship training class. Help them feel as comfortable as possible. Explain how you too are a disciple.
>
> As a Christian, we are automatically part of God's worldwide and eternal family. The Church, God's family, should be thought of both as worldwide and local (John 1:11-13; Eph 2:19-22).
>
> ***Overview of the training.***
>
> – If possible, allow 2 hours for each session.
>
> – If absent, they are expected to notify you ahead of time.
>
> – They will be expected to complete their assignments, including memory verses.

You belong!
THE CHURCH

❖ Overview of the 3xE Chart *<= One session*

- ### Exaltation *<= Two sessions*
    - *1) The need and place of true worship.*
    - *2) The ways to protect your worship.*

- ### Edification *<= Two sessions*
    - *1) How to grow as a Christian.*
    - *2) Our responsibility and ability to strengthen other Christians.*

- ### Evangelism *<= Two sessions*
    - *1) The urgent need to share the gospel.*
    - *2) Sharing the gospel through your testimony.*

❖ Purpose and Goals of Your Church

The Church has been called by God to Exaltation (Psalm 100), Edification (Eph 4:7-16; Acts 2:42) and Evangelism (Mat 28:18-20; John 17:18). Explain how your local church is carrying Christ's purposes and mission statement.

Also share some specific examples as to how God is now using people in your church (besides the pastors if possible) to help others grow and proclaim God's truth.

❖ Fitting into the Family

Overview of some of the functions of the different purposes of your church's activities.

See how many different groups are operating in your Church.

Cell groups
Fellowship groups
Bible studies
Youth Fellowship
Prayer meeting
Worship services
Door-to-door
Visitation
Mission committee
Choir
etc.

Identify a few of their goals. (Rom 12:1-21)

What problems are they facing in meeting these goals? (Heb 10:24-25)

Where can <u>YOU</u> be INVOLVED?

Share how you are involved in the local church and how your participation has changed over time since you have become a Christian. Let him/her know that God has saved them to make him/her part of the local church.

❖ Understand Your Leaders

Draw a diagram of how the leaders of your church relate to each other and to the local church (organizational structure).

Each local church has its own distinct diagram. Draw out the organizational structure of your church ahead of time. Draw one for them. Have them copy it into their booklet.

The Elder Board
Includes both pastors and elders

The Church Council
Includes both elders and deacons

The Church
We encourage every Christian to join an organizational church!

❖ **Good habits you should start:**

1. Buy a Bible and have a daily devotion time with God

2. Regularly attend Sunday worship

3. Join a small/community group

In conclusion:

- *Pray together for the Church.*
- *Assign the homework.*
- *Confirm next session's time and place.*
- *Make sure they know how to find verses in their Bible!*

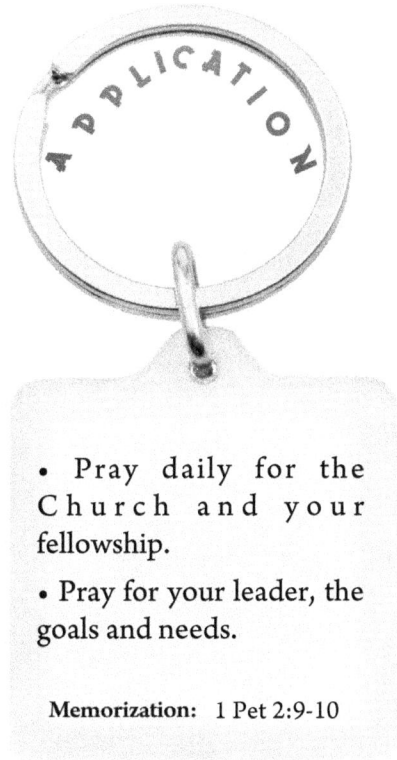

• Pray daily for the Church and your fellowship.

• Pray for your leader, the goals and needs.

Memorization: 1 Pet 2:9-10

Session #2 The Duty and Delight of Exalting God

The purpose of this session is to help the disciplee realize the need, privilege, and means of worshiping God in their daily lives (Deut 6:4-7,13; Mat 4:10). Regularly refer to the 3xE diagram.

At the beginning of the session:

- *Welcome them with a smile.*
- *Check homework.*
- *Open in prayer.*

❖ Defining Worship

Worship is the common act of service offered unto God in which we delightfully give to Him what rightly belongs to Him including our adoration, honor, and obedience.

Our lives revolve around the Lord.

> *Share a 'living' or practical definition of worship such as: "Living our lives in conformity to the will of God." Connect the chart to the discussion here as well as in each session.*

- **Worship regularly together as a church (John 4:24).**

- **Worship routinely together as a family.**

- **Worship daily as an individual.**

‾ *Practically share how church worship functions.*

‾ *Attending worship services is not just physically showing up but consciously exalting our Lord. Worship is not an option (Heb 10:25)!*

‾ *Conducting/participating in family worship (Deut 6).*

- Engaging in conscious personal worship during daily devotions (Heb 8:10-11; Ps 139).

❖ Motives for our Worship

How would you measure your enthusiasm to praise and worship God in your life?

- *God lives! Our true motives come from our understanding of how great God is and how He treats us far better than we deserve!*

- *Psalm 100: "He is our Shepherd; we His sheep."*

- *Psalm 119:68*

Don't forget to share what you have been learning recently about worship and other experiences with the Lord!

❖ Knowing the God We Worship

SOVEREIGN

HOLY

JUST

WRATHFUL

LOVING

KIND

MERCIFUL

GRACIOUS

GOOD

OMNISCIENT (ALL-KNOWING)

OMNIPRESENT (EVERYWHERE)

OMNIPOTENT (ALL-POWERFUL)

RIGHTEOUS

Some of God's attributes (characteristics)

Make sure you write your thoughts down!

Studying and worshipping together

- *Choose a characteristic of God (see the list)*

- *Find verses in the Bible to help them better understand this attribute. Familiarize them with the concordance & cross-references in the Bible if necessary.*

- *Explain how worship is not only telling God about His greatness but also properly responding to His person as revealed in Scriptures.*

> Go through a Psalm or passage detecting God's person and power.
>
> Sample passages: Psalm 145:1-13 | Psalm 103 | Psalm 139

How to study

- *Discuss how that attribute of God should affect your lives.*
- *Pray in a worshipful way (together if possible, but it's not necessary).*
- *Share with them how these thoughts can be part of their spiritual journal.*

- **Knowing God's greatness enables us to properly honor Him.**

- **Understanding God's holiness helps us to be like Him.**

- **Embracing God's salvation brings humility and joy to our worship.**

In conclusion:

- *Try to answer any related questions.*
- *Assign the homework.*
- *Make the study and conversation as deep as they can comfortably handle.*

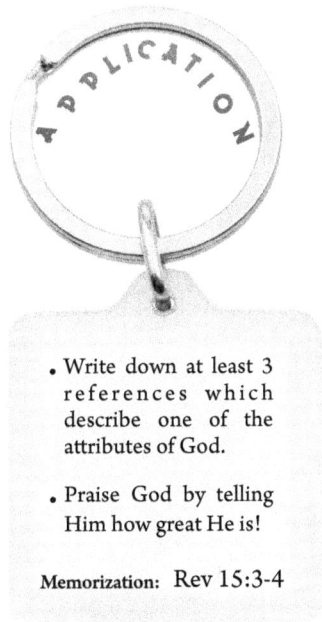

APPLICATION

- Write down at least 3 references which describe one of the attributes of God.

- Praise God by telling Him how great He is!

Memorization: Rev 15:3-4

Session #3 Preserving Our Worship

The purpose of this session is to help the disciples to realize the need and know-how of preserving the continuity of worship known as communing with Christ.

- *Welcome them with a smile.*
- *Go over the homework and review last week's session.*
- *Review 3xE diagram and introduce today's session.*

❖ Review the Truths of Salvation

Don't be afraid to review some basics! Faithful Christian discipleship involves preserving our relationship with Christ.

· Salvation through Jesus Christ alone

Walk through the bridge diagram below. You could ask if they know how to share the gospel with another person. If so, ask them to tell it. If not, go ahead and show them how, and then have them repeat it.

· Sin's Heavy Burden

- Guilty feelings (Ro 4:6-9) versus legal guilt (Rom 5:12-21; 3:9)

- Gaining cleansing (I John 1:9) ; *Wrong actions (James 4:17; 1 John 3:4)*

- Overcoming temptation (I Cor 10:13) ; *Inner corruption (Rom 7:17)*

God can be trusted in all circumstances!
Just don't put yourself in a bad situation.

· Security of Believer

Once saved, always saved. Once His child, always part of God's family. But affirmation of this fact should not only come from past confession but present commitment.

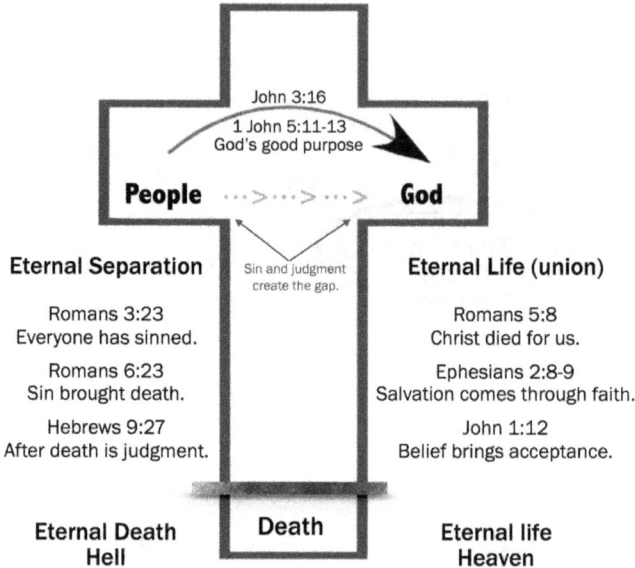

John 3:16
1 John 5:11-13
God's good purpose

People ···>···>···> **God**

Eternal Separation   Sin and judgment   **Eternal Life (union)**
                               create the gap.

Romans 3:23   Romans 5:8
Everyone has sinned.   Christ died for us.

Romans 6:23   Ephesians 2:8-9
Sin brought death.   Salvation comes through faith.

Hebrews 9:27   John 1:12
After death is judgment.   Belief brings acceptance.

Eternal Death   **Death**   **Eternal life**
Hell   **Heaven**

❖ Practically Make Jesus Lord of Your Life

John 2:24-25; Mat 7:22-23

Jesus is the Lord of our lives, but we must affirm this truth by obeying His demands/commands. You might mention that the reason Christians worship each Sunday is to pause one day each week to remember the Lord with all the other saints.

❖ Use Your God-given resources

· Baptism and Communion (Lord's Supper)

Review the significance of these two ordinances.

· Word of God

You could review how the Bible, prayer and worship fit into the Christian's life.

· Prayer

Don't assume the basics! Tell them how to start a prayer, what to say, how to end and the purpose for each. A good example is the Lord's prayer (Mat 6:9-13).

3xE Discipleship - Discipler's Version

3xE Discipleship - Discipler's Version   31

- **Worship Service**

  Worship has nothing to do with being entertained and feeling good, but it does have everything to do with giving God the attention, glory, and honor He deserves. Faithful attendance is important.

- **Cell (Small) Group**

  Strongly encourage them to be part of a small group that meets during the week for accountability and community. Help them over any barriers to this.

- **Giving**

  Could use 2 Cor 8:1-9 to show the joy of giving and our responsibility to share what God has given to the church and others.

❖ Confront Issues that Challenge Your Loyalty

- **Worship versus worry**

Worry dethrones God and elevates problems.

- *Mention a couple problems people often have (worry, anger, etc.).*

- *God is sufficient for salvation.*

- *God is sufficient for any difficult circumstances (Ps 23).*

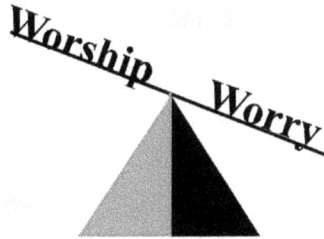

Matthew 6:33

- *Share an example from your own life of how the Lord helped you.*

- *Pray together over one or more problems Christians face, and more specifically that the disciple face.*

In conclusion,

- *Assign homework below.*

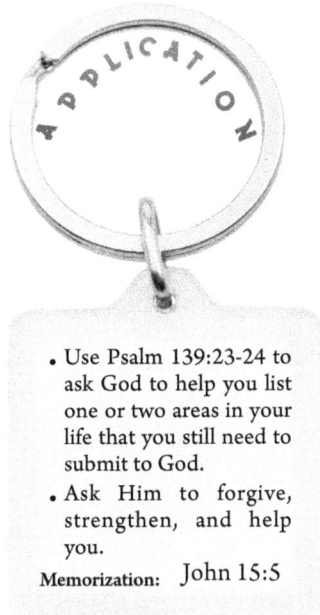

- Use Psalm 139:23-24 to ask God to help you list one or two areas in your life that you still need to submit to God.
- Ask Him to forgive, strengthen, and help you.

Memorization: John 15:5

Session #4 Personal Edification

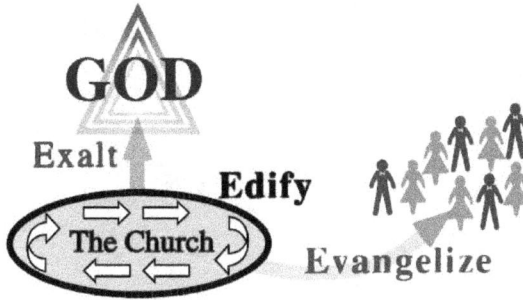

- *Welcome them with a smile.*
- *Go over the homework/memory verses and review last week's session.*
- *Review 3xE diagram and introduce Edification's 2 sections.*

❖ The Definition of Edification

Edification means "to build up," and "to strengthen"; it is a special process whereby a Christian grows spiritually. Change is to be expected!

> *God is changing each Christian so that he can glorify God through:*
>
> *1) Living an obedient life with sincere motivation (Eph 4:1-3)*
> *2) Serving other Christians (Eph 4:12)*
> *3) Bringing the gospel to non-Christians (Eph 3:8-12).*

❖ The Means of Edification

- *Describe the regular means of edifying yourself (Col 1:9-12; 2 Peter 1).*
- *Check to see if they own a Bible and hymn/song book.*
- *Have them circle the activities in which they have participated in the box below.*
- *Explain activities that are unclear.*

❖ What is holding you back?

Satan and his demons	The world with its lust	Our flesh–self-oriented nature
Eph 6:10-13 A real spiritual warfare **Satan vs. God's ways**	**I John 2:15-17** A real power struggle: **The world vs. God's ways**	**Rom 8:5-6; Gal 5:16-25** A real fight: Flesh ◄──► Spirit
• *Satan is clever.* • *Don't always blame him.* • *Never underestimate him.* • *Pray always.* • *False idea:* • *–Satan doesn't exist*	• *A battle with our surroundings.* • *It's not neutral!* • *The world lures us.* • *The world is a wicked force with an intent and practices opposed to God's way and kingdom (Rom 12:2).*	• *Explain what the flesh and Spirit natures mean.* • *Give examples of both.* • *Flesh no longer has authority or power over us unless we willingly submit to those desires.* • *The Holy Spirit rules us as we submit to His purpose and design.*

Tendency to Backslide
and ways to come back quickly!

Because of the forces waging war against Christians, we can and sometimes fall into sin. We even, at times, remain in sin. This is called backsliding. For a genuine Christian, this is always temporary. However, if one does not come back to the Lord, it shows that he/she never was a genuine Christian in the first place (1 John 2:19; 5:4). We must always quickly come back to the Lord through confession of our sin (1 John 1:9-2:2) and find acceptance in His forgiveness and restoration. Satan wants to keep us down, discouraged, and ineffective. Christ has made it so that we can come back immediately. Although the consequences of our sin might be terrible (eg. must go to jail), the Lord can and does restore our Father-child relationship with Him (Rom 4:6-8).

Destroying strongholds

Strongholds are areas of our lives that we have given up hope in. Seek God to take them all down, one by one, just like Joshua took the land of Canaan, city by city, king by king.

In conclusion,

• *Go over one section of Psalm 119 and identify some truths from it as an example of edification. Do it with him/her.*

• *For homework, have them do another section and write down edifying thoughts on paper.*

• *Pray out these truths with both thanksgiving and requests.*

• *Assign them to do this for their homework.*

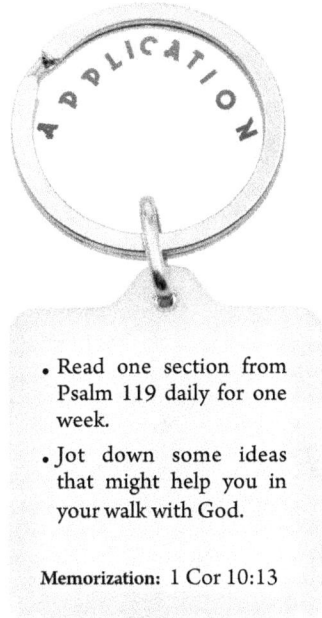

. Read one section from Psalm 119 daily for one week.

. Jot down some ideas that might help you in your walk with God.

Memorization: 1 Cor 10:13

Session #5 Edifying Others

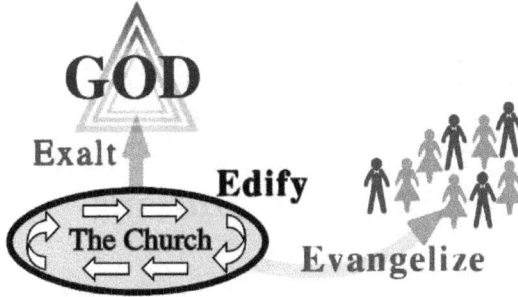

- *Welcome them with a smile.*

- *Go over the homework and emphasize the importance of edification.*

- *Review 3xE diagram (importance of church, duty of worship, preserving our worship) and then these two sessions on edification.*

❖ The reasons we edify others

· You are part of the church, the body of Christ.

> *Explain why edification is necessary to all believers and how each one plays a role in it.*

· You are responsible to care for others.

> *All Christians make up the body of Christ (1 John 1:3, Rom 6:3-4; 12:5).*

· Others are responsible to care for you.

> *(Eph 4:1-4, 12)*

"Love one another"

Each Christian is commanded to live a life rooted in service to one another with the very love of God.
(1 John 4:7-11)

· According to God's design, we NEED the help of others.

- *(Eph 4:11-13; Gal 6:2,6,10; 1 Cor 12:12-27)*

- *Remind them how today's emphasis on individualism and rights goes counter to the teaching of the cross.*

❖ Small groups
A great way to edify one another

A small group is a weekly gathering of 5-8 people who form a community in which to experience God, spiritually grow in relationship to others, and reach out to the lost (Exaltation, Edification, Evangelism).

❖ Practical Ways of Edifying Others

Have the disciple list some practical ways to edify others.
The principles we use to strengthen our Christian lives are the same principles we employ to strengthen others (review prior lessons). Start off with a personal example. Continue by picking out at least five more items from Romans 12:9-21.

1.   6.

2.   7.

3.   8.

4.   9.

5.   10.

❖ A Special Way of Edifying Others

• *Briefly explain spiritual gifts (1 Cor 12:4-6).*

• *Each Christian has at least one gift (1 Cor 12:7).*

• *The purpose of gifts is to serve God by edifying others (1 Cor 12:7, 25).*

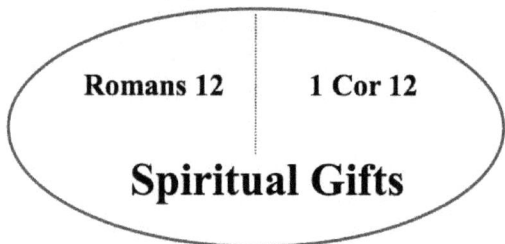

Romans 12	1 Cor 12

Spiritual Gifts

• *Ask them if they know what their spiritual gift(s) is/are.*

• *Share one spiritual gift God has given you and how you use it.*

• *Remind them that it sometimes takes time to discover spiritual gifts so they should not worry about not knowing right now.*

• *Basic lesson: God designed them to serve others and be strengthened by others.*

In conclusion,

• *Be practical.*

• *Give an example of how you edified someone this past week or how someone edified you.*

• *Ask for questions and discuss this as time permits.*

• *Pray together, thanking the Lord as to how others helped you and for insight in seeing how you can see and meet the needs of others.*

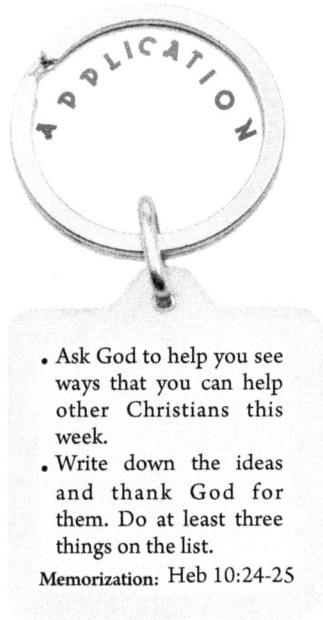

. Ask God to help you see ways that you can help other Christians this week.

. Write down the ideas and thank God for them. Do at least three things on the list.

Memorization: Heb 10:24-25

Session #6 Evangelism

- *Warmly welcome them.*
- *Review the homework/memorization and share a recent personal example of how God edified you.*
- *Review 3xE diagram (Exalt, Edify, Evangelize). Introduce Evangelism with the above diagram.*

❖ The Definition of Evangelism

Evangelism is the spreading of God's truth, the plan of salvation known as the gospel, to non-Christians through words and deeds. One beggar showing another beggar where to find food.

> *Briefly define evangelism (broad and narrow definitions).*
>
> *• Broad: Evangelism involves sharing our testimony and life with others, like Daniel in Persia. People know we take certain stands because of our faith.*
>
> *• Narrow: Involves speaking or communicating God's saving truth clearly to others. It is more common to have opportunity to share a special aspect of the gospel rather than all gospel truths at once.*

❖ The Need for Evangelism

1. The command of Jesus

2. The reality of hell

3. The lostness of mankind

4. The supremacy of worship

Evangelism is a critical part of the Christian's life. God commanded us to spread the gospel (Mat 28:17-20; Acts 1:8), and so we have included this as part of the 3xE diagram. Missions is the whole program, the big picture; evangelism one primary means by which to fulfill the mission that our Lord gave us.

Hell is real.

•*Discuss the reality of hell (Mk 9:47-48; Mt 10:28).*

•*People live under Satan's power (Col 1:13).*

•*Without Christ people live under God's wrath (John 3:36; Rom 5:12-21).*

❖ The Means of Evangelism

✓ Live a godly life (1 Thes 1:7-9)

> *An upright life is crucial (if in sin, confess and apologize).*

✓ Know the Gospel (See session #3)

> *Review what makes a person a Christian and possible ways to explain it to non-Christians.*

✓ Be proactive in sharing

> *Personal evangelism is difficult for many people, but we must do what the Lord has asked. He provides boldness as we seek Him.*

✓ Convinced of God's truth (1 Thes 1:5)

> *Remember that God changes people in His time and not in our timing.*

✓ Pray for opportunities, wisdom and courage

> – *Paul did this in Eph 6:19-20.*
>
> – *There are many means to pass God's truth on.*

❖ Answering Difficult Questions

When you don't know a good answer, just say so. If an answer is important to them, tell them that you can study up on the issue. But many questions are distracting smoke screens, where they care more about justifying something than they do an answer. Keep your focus on presenting the gospel, which you do know.

In conclusion *(make sure you keep to your time),*

- *Share briefly how you became a Christian.*
- *Ask them how they became a Christian.*
- *Assign homework. Don't forget to encourage them!*
- *Putting the testimony on their computer might be better than writing it in this notebook. But do have them bring you a copy next week!*

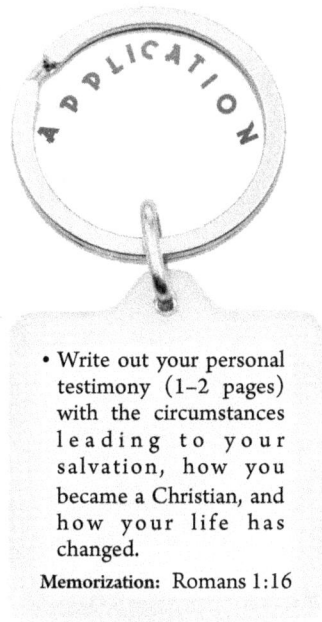

- Write out your personal testimony (1–2 pages) with the circumstances leading to your salvation, how you became a Christian, and how your life has changed.

Memorization: Romans 1:16

•

Session #7 A Personal Evangelism Strategy

· *Welcome them with a smile.*

· *Review the whole 3xE diagram.*

· *Have them share 1 or 2 things that they are learning from this lesson.*

· *Review their testimony. Be honest.*

❖ God has placed you into circles of relationships

These relationships are the places you can naturally share the gospel. *Oikos* is the Greek word depicting these natural "household" relationships.

   1. Personal

   2. Extended

   3. Potential

Do you have meaningful relationships with non-Christians?

❖ God has given you talents, interests, and skills to build bridges to the lost.

Which "bridge" can you use to create opportunities?

❖ There are different level of responsiveness among non-Christians.

You must know your audience to reach them.

1. Seekers

2. Open to the message

3. Open to the messenger

4. Distorted or unaware

5. Hostile

6. Churched unbelievers

❖ My Testimony

The best way to conclude these sessions is for the discipler to take the disciplee somewhere to share the gospel with someone. You can go to a park or visit a new person from church and share your testimony. The point is that you set the example so that they watch, learn, and become more eager to join in God's work.

Have several testimonies that focus on different kinds of people and situations. I suggest having different length testimonies: 1, 3, 5, and 15 minutes for different occasions that can open up.

✓ What was my life like before I came to know Jesus?

_____

_____

_____

_____

_____

_____

_____

✓ **How did I become a Christian?**

_____

_____

_____

_____

_____

_____

✓ **How is my life different now that I am walking with Jesus**

_____

_____

_____

_____

_____

_____

_____

_____

_____

_____

_____

❖ Any Questions

Answer any questions they might have.

✓ On evangelism?

Share how to use their testimony to share the gospel with another person. "I was like that once, but something changed my life..." You can also use other experiences that reflect the way God's truth noticeably changed your life.

✓ On the 3xE chart?

See how well they understand the basics of this discipleship program. Remember we are not just looking at a person's knowledge but at how that knowledge impacts their lives.

✓ On training others?

Now it is your turn to join the millions of Christ's disciples throughout the world by being a faithful disciple maker.

· *Explain the need for self-discipline to disciple others.*

· *Explain your willingness to help.*

· *Encourage their faithfulness in the church.*

· *Remind them of the great need for discipleship. The purpose of this booklet is to make sure people know the basics. Other stages follow this first stage (See The Flow diagram in Appendix 1).*

· *Explain how you will seek an occasion to train another person with them so that they can gain confidence in discipling others.*

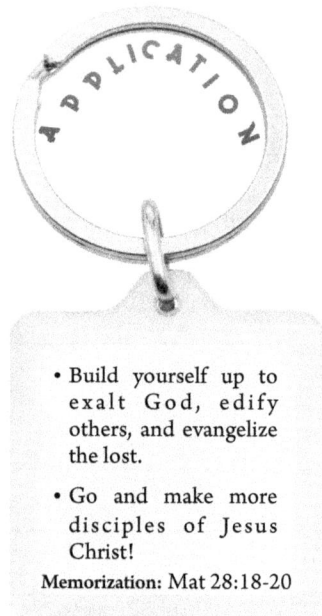

• Build yourself up to exalt God, edify others, and evangelize the lost.

• Go and make more disciples of Jesus Christ!

Memorization: Mat 28:18-20

Appendix 1: The Flow Diagram

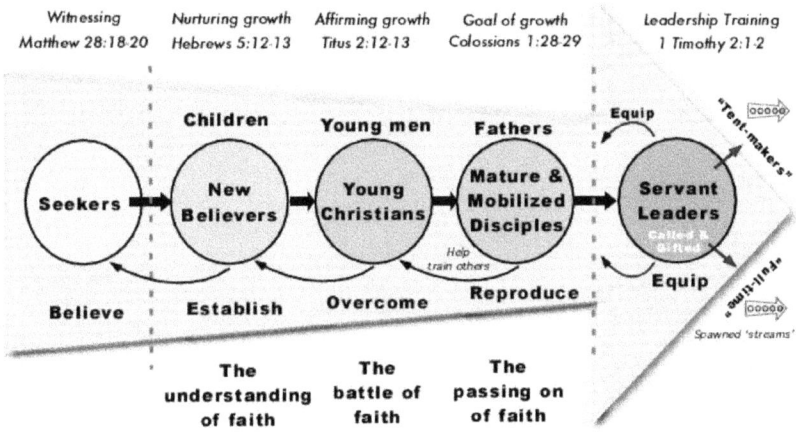

THE FLOW
TRACING CHRISTIAN GROWTH
1 JOHN 2:12-14

Witnessing	Nurturing growth	Affirming growth	Goal of growth	Leadership Training
Matthew 28:18-20	Hebrews 5:12-13	Titus 2:12-13	Colossians 1:28-29	1 Timothy 2:1-2

Children   Young men   Fathers   Equip   "Tent-makers"

Seekers → New Believers → Young Christians → Mature & Mobilized Disciples → Servant Leaders

Help train others   Called & Gifted   Equip   "Multi-ply"

Believe   Establish   Overcome   Reproduce   Spawned 'streams'

The understanding of faith   The battle of faith   The passing on of faith

Your Notes

About the Authors

Rev. Paul J. Bucknell, an active author and international instructor, has written more than twenty books on pertinent Christian training topics. His books are written with the conviction that the more we build our lives on the truth of God's Word, the stronger and more vibrant our faith and lives will be. Paul's international training seminars take God's Word and apply the truth therein to different aspects of Christian living for pastors and Christian leaders. As founder of Biblical Foundations for Freedom, Paul provides printed and digital media, along with video training courses and a website ministry. Paul with his wife, Linda, have eight children and delight in their four grandchildren.

Rev. Hugo Cheng, a church planter and a pastor, has a great passion to see churches become effective in discipling men and women into mature Christians. He has trained many healthy disciples and disciple makers, as well as raised up many effective church leaders in the last 20 plus years. Hugo and his wife, Heather, have 6 children.